Victorian Scroll Saw Patterns

Patrick Spielman

Art by Dirk Boelman, The Art Factory

Sterling Publishing Co., Inc.   New York

Library of Congress Cataloging-in-Publication Data

Spielman, Patrick E.
   Victorian scroll saw patterns / by Patrick Spielman.
      p.   cm.
   Includes index.
   1. Jig saws.   2. Woodwork.   3. Decoration and ornament—Victorian
style.   I. title.
   TT186.S678   1990
   745.51—dc20   90-37344
                                                                     CIP

Edited by Timothy Nolan

10 9 8 7 6 5 4 3 2

Copyright © 1990 by Patrick Spielman
Published by Sterling Publishing Company, Inc.
387 Park Avenue South, New York, NY 10016
Distributed in Canada by Sterling Publishing
% Canadian Manda Group, P. O. Box 920, Station U
Toronto, Ontario, Canada M8Z 5P9
Distributed in Great Britain and Europe by Cassell PLC
Villiers House, 41/47 Strand, London WC2N 5JE, England
Distributed in Australia by Capricorn Ltd.
P. O. Box 665, Lane Cove, NSW 2066
Manufactured in the United States of America
All rights reserved
Sterling ISBN 0-8069-7294-7 Paper

Contents

Acknowledgments

I am extremely grateful to Dirk Boelman of The Art Factory for his many creative talents, tireless efforts, and exceptional skills in preparing the finished art for all of the patterns. His fine line work, drawn in smooth flowing curves and very precise detailing, make these patterns a joy and delight to cut with any scroll saw. The thin lines (and helpful shading accents) allow you to follow them more easily and far more accurately than would be possible with most other scroll saw patterns available.

The assistance of Sherri Spielman Valitchka in shading some of the patterns is also appreciated.

Thanks to the outstanding work of these two key individuals, I am very pleased and proud to present these beautiful patterns, of unequaled quality, to scroll-sawing crafts people everywhere.

Metric Conversion Chart

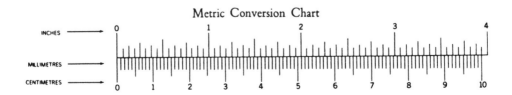

Introduction

Some of the most popular scroll-sawing patterns of the late 1800s are redrawn and reproduced in this book. Most of these highly detailed and ornate patterns were originally created by early scroll saw masters. Included here, with some of our own creations and adaptations, are works published in the 1870s by then-famous names, including Arthur Hope, Henry Williams, and Orlando Ware. Where necessary, their patterns have been slightly changed or altered to make them more adaptable to present-day scroll-sawing techniques. These refinements were made by Dirk Boelman, probably the most talented and productive designer and developer of fine fretwork patterns working today.

The majority of the old pattern designs is virtually unchanged from the original profiles. Some larger patterns are extended across three to four adjoining pages, and other large symmetrical patterns are given here in just quarter or half patterns. These are designated with central lines where patterns should be folded or flipped to form the complete, full pattern (Illus. 1).

Although many of the design profiles are essentially unchanged, all of the early patterns were redrawn. In many cases the old-style full, solid black patterns were converted to new patterns with fine, crisp outlines with line or grey shading. This makes the patterns much easier to saw accurately because the saw blade contrasts better to the pattern and does not as readily blend into the background of the pattern itself.

To conserve space, some of the more obvious patterns have been eliminated, including rectangular patterns for box bottoms and liners, and shelves for wall brackets. Also omitted are half-circular and quarter-circular-shaped patterns that comprise the wall shelf and/or corner shelves for various bracket projects.

Most of the old patterns given in this book were probably originally sawn from thin solid woods $\frac{1}{8}$ inch to $\frac{5}{16}$ inch thick, depending upon the nature of the project. With today's modern scroll saws, thicker materials are now more easily cut, and this option will make certain projects, such as the silhouettes and picture or mirror frames, more interesting.

Because of the delicacy of some of the very ornate and fragile pieces once they are cut out, it will be easier to finish-sand the surfaces before sawing. A good scroll saw should cut the sawn surfaces forming the profile edges so smooth that they will require very little if any subsequent sanding.

Many of the patterns are so highly detailed that they will require very small "saw gates" or blade-entry holes that can only be threaded with fine pinless blades; the most

Illus. 1. Some patterns for large projects such as this mirror or picture frame are given full-size, but only in a one-page half or quarter pattern which needs to be repeated and/or flipped to make the complete, full pattern.

Illus. 2. The plant hanger project (pages 149–153) requires six identical pieces. Saw all from ¼-inch-thick material. They can all be stacked and cut at once as shown with one of the many new precision-cutting scroll saws now available.

delicate cuttings will require the fine No. 2, 3, or 4 blade. Most patterns can be cut with medium blades (No's. 5–7) and some of the larger projects should be cut with No. 8 to No. 11 blades. Always use the biggest possible blade, but do not sacrifice the ability to cut fine detail or the smoothness of the cut surface. Thicker materials will require heavier blades, so plan accordingly.

One of the biggest problems with scroll sawing is developing patterns and transferring them to the workpiece. Since all the patterns in this book are given in recommended-size versions, no enlargements or

reductions are actually necessary unless some special size is desired. In such cases the easiest and quickest way to make size changes is with the assistance of an office copier that has enlarging and reducing capabilities. Otherwise, the old process of drawing grids can be employed, but this is often time-consuming and not very accurate.

Use the office copy machine to make an exact copy of the patterns you intend to saw. The copies can then be temporarily bonded directly onto the surface of the workpiece. Use a brush-on rubber cement or a temporary bonding spray adhesive. I personally prefer the spray adhesive. Simply spray a very light mist of adhesive to the back of the pattern copy (do not spray on wood) and wait just a few seconds; then press the pattern onto the wood with your hand. Saw out the piece following exactly the same lines of the pattern. This technique results in far more accurate finished cuts (with smoother curves, etc.), and just more overall sawing pleasure.

A machine-copied pattern peels off the workpiece cleanly and easily after the sawing operations are completed. Temporary mounting spray adhesives are inexpensive and available from art, craft, and photography retail suppliers. Just be sure you get one that states "temporary bond" on the can.

If you can, avoid the old method of tracing the pattern from the book and then transferring the traced pattern to the workpiece with carbon paper. If you must do it that way, use graphite paper. It is cleaner, less greasy, and the image it leaves is more easily removed with light sanding.

If you use rubber cement to bond a machine-copied pattern to the workpiece, a little more care is required. Do not brush on too heavy a coat. If some cement remains on the wood after peeling off the pattern, it can be removed by rubbing it off with your fingers (do *not* use solvents). Conversely, when temporary bond spray adhesive is properly applied no residue remains on the wood surface. In either case you may want to *very carefully* lightly sand the surfaces with fine-grit paper (180 grit or smoother) before finishing.

Don't forget to employ the technique of *stack-sawing* two or more layers at a time to duplicate parts exactly. Stacking multiple layers (*gang* or *plural sawing*) is a good way to increase production and to make several cutouts all at one time, depending upon individual thicknesses (Illus. 2). Today ultra-thin plywoods are available to permit stacking many layers. However, you may want to use thin solid woods, as in earlier times, to create more authentic and historically accurate reproductions of these patterns, because plywood was not invented or widely used until the 1940s.

The selection of patterns provided here is, for the most part, an authentic reflection of scroll-sawing work done at the peak of the Victorian era. The nostalgic silhouettes depicting adult life styles and child's play, the ornate shelves, picture or mirror frames, filigree baskets, decorative boxes, crosses, numbers and letters, and many other decorative and useful patterns should provide scroll-sawing challenges and complement Victorian decorating schemes—a trend rapidly gaining in popularity.

I would be remiss if I didn't mention two related and helpful books: *Scroll Saw Fretwork Techniques and Projects* (Sterling Publishing Co., New York, 1990) and *Scroll Saw Fretwork Patterns* (Sterling Publishing Co., New York, 1989). Both are co-authored with my friend and colleague, James Reidle. *Techniques* offers a study in the historical development of fretwork, as well as the tools, techniques, materials, and project styles that have evolved over the past 130 years. The book also covers some modern scroll-sawing machines and current state-of-the-art fretwork and fine-scroll-sawing techniques. Those books, along with these Victorian patterns, will make this fascinating class of woodworking more fun and at the same time faster and a whole lot easier than it ever was at any time in the Victorian era.

Silhouettes

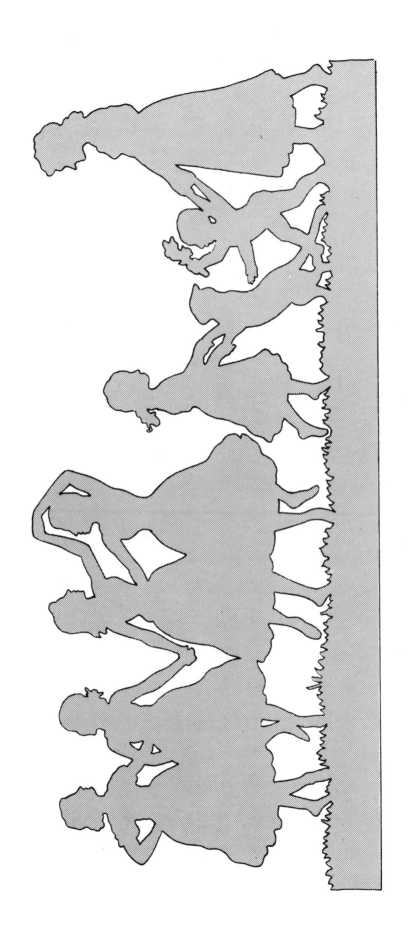

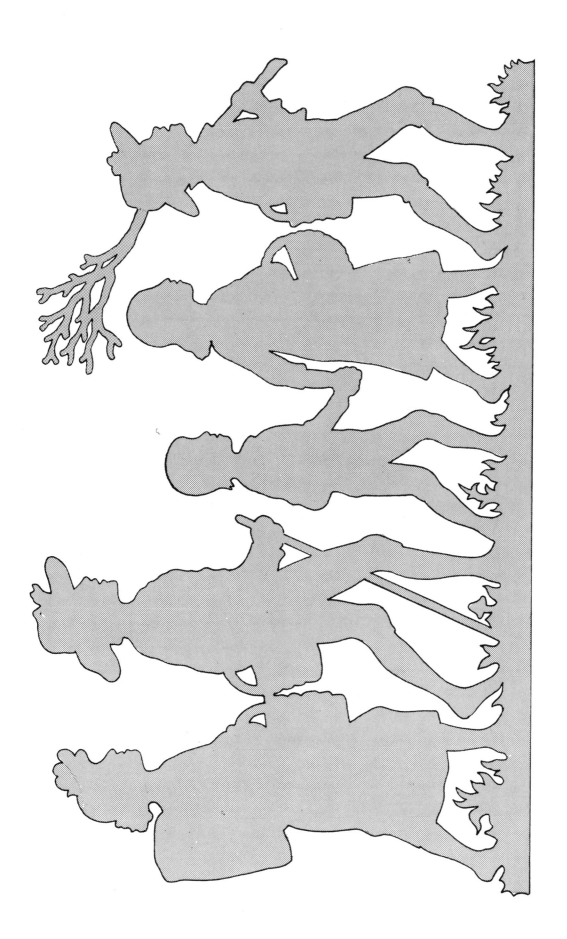

*Silhouettes sawn
from ⅜-inch plywood
prepainted with
a dull black aerosol
before sawing.*

20

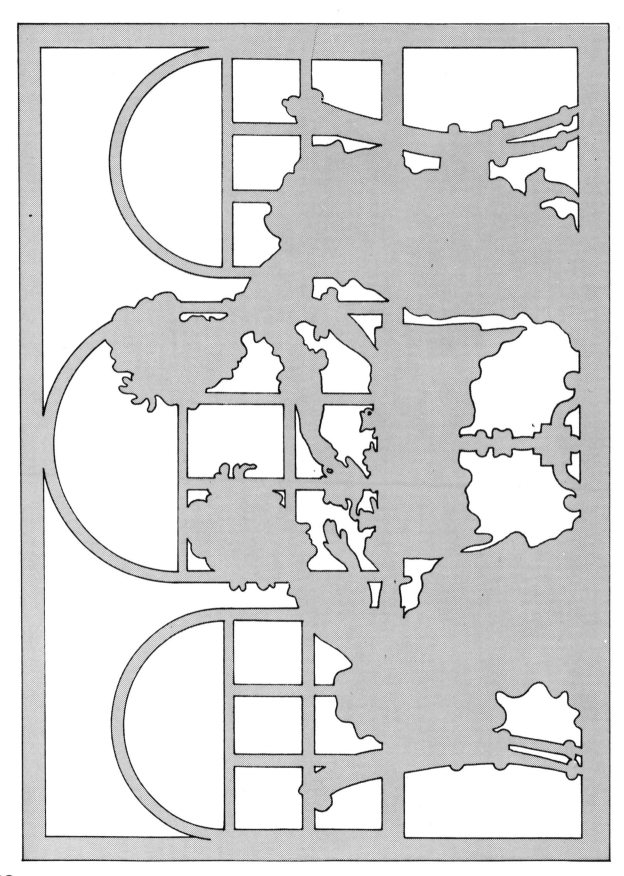

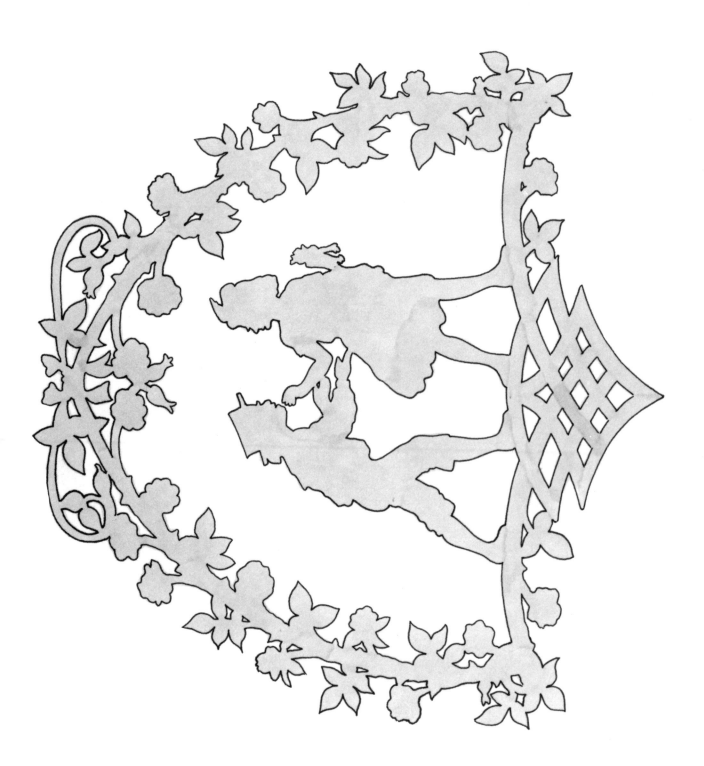

Numbers

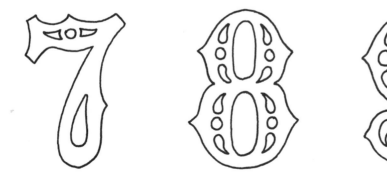

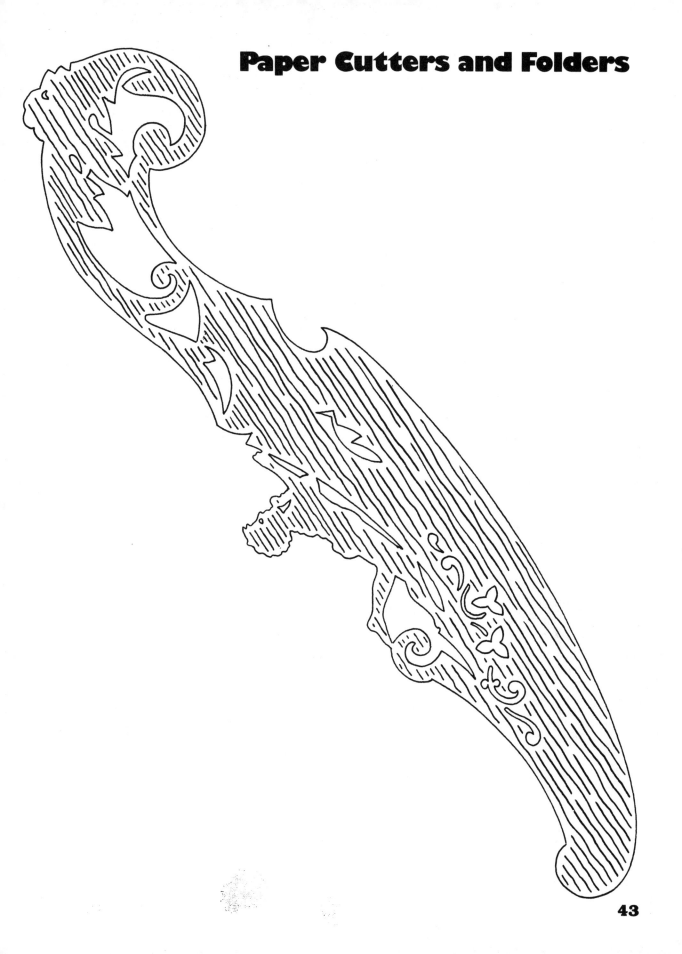

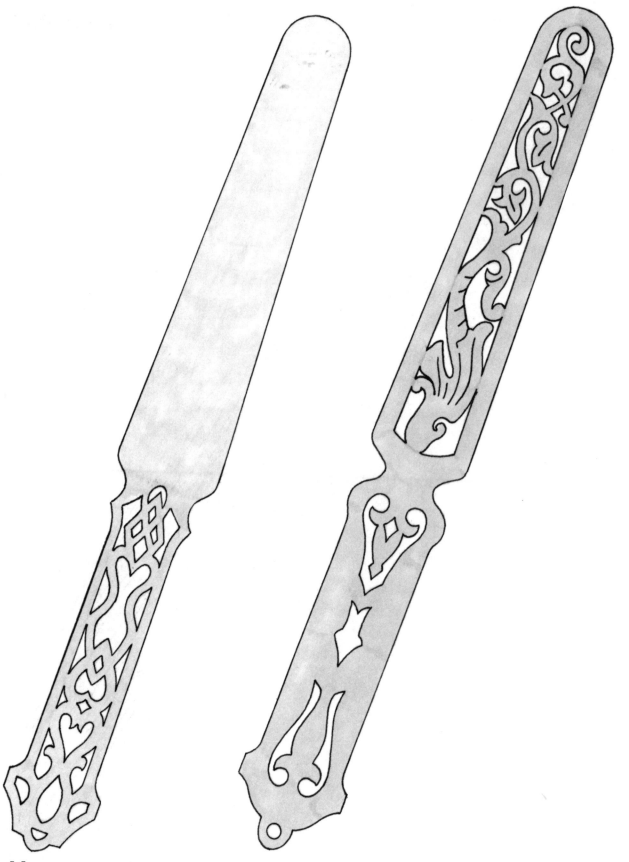

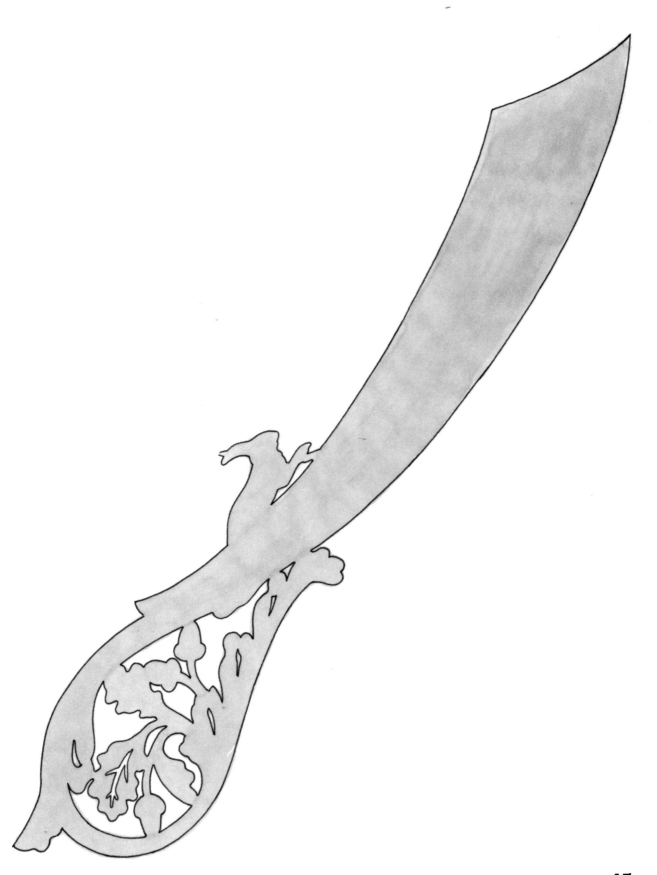

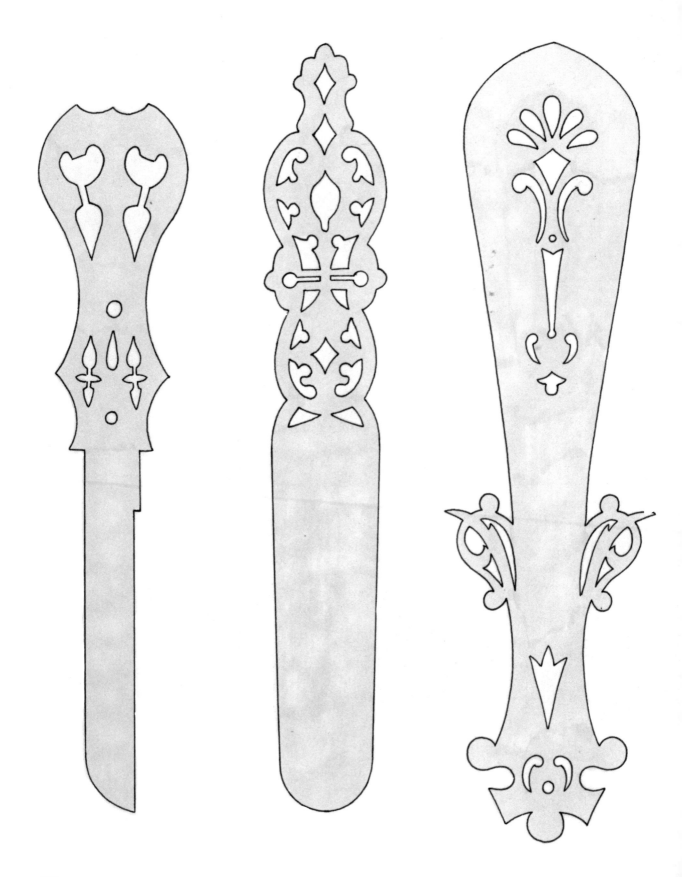

Cross sawn from ¾-inch-thick mahogany.

Wheelbarrow Receivers

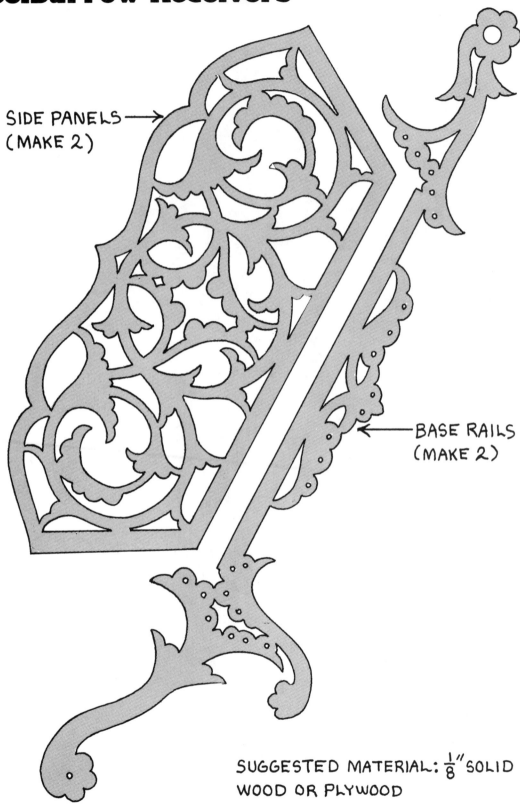

SIDE PANELS
(MAKE 2)

BASE RAILS
(MAKE 2)

SUGGESTED MATERIAL: $\frac{1}{8}''$ SOLID
WOOD OR PLYWOOD

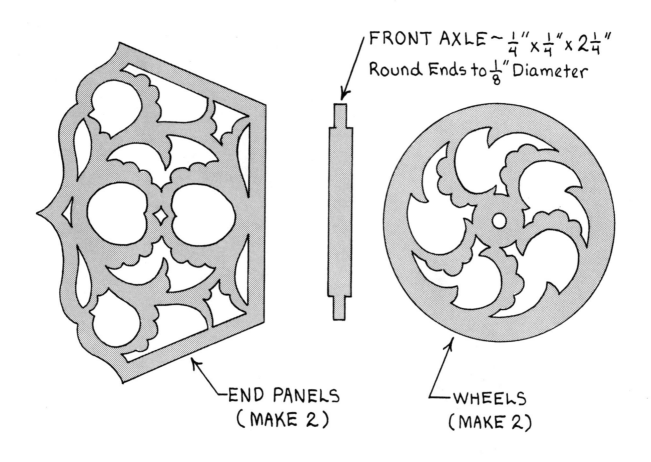

FRONT AXLE ~ $\frac{1}{4}'' \times \frac{1}{4}'' \times 2\frac{1}{4}''$
Round Ends to $\frac{1}{8}''$ Diameter

END PANELS
(MAKE 2)

WHEELS
(MAKE 2)

BASE PANEL

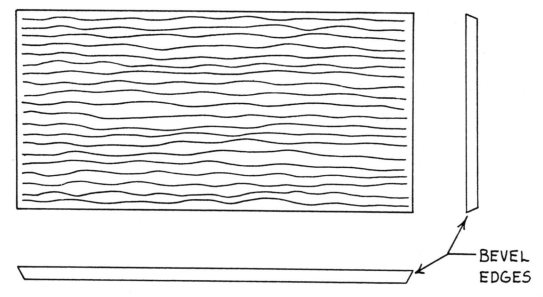

BEVEL
EDGES

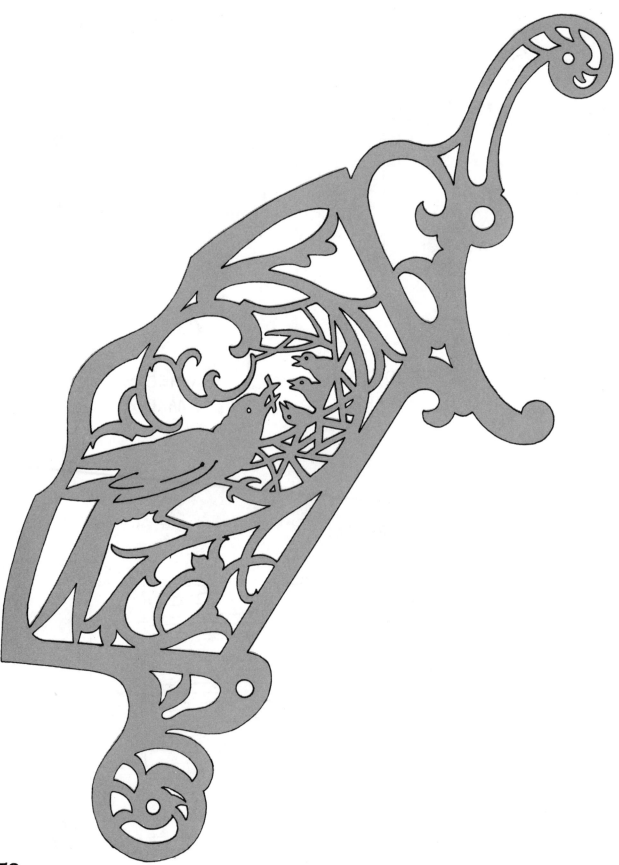

52

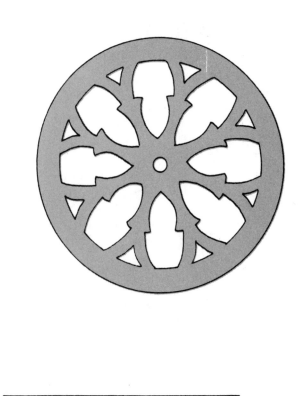

Welcome Sign

A

B

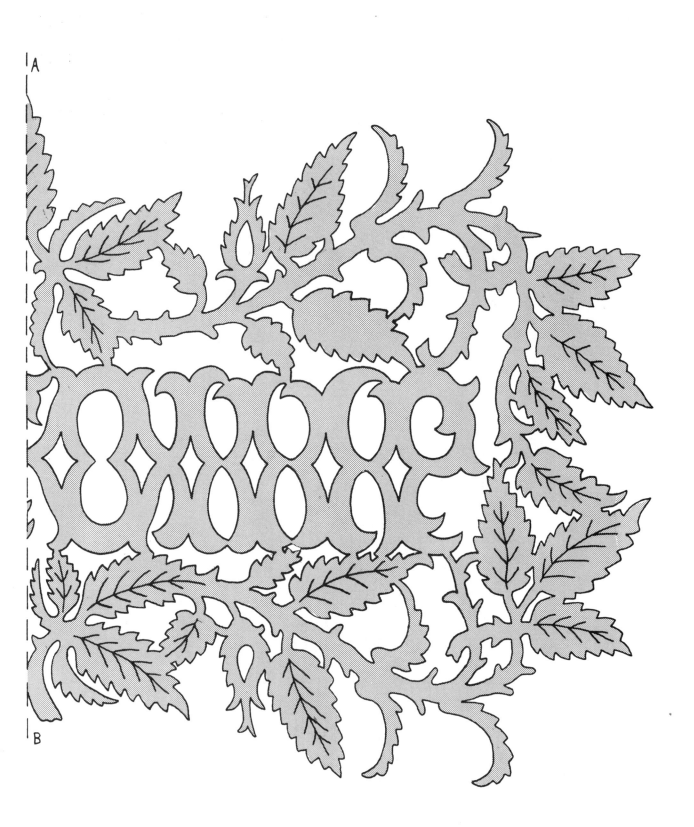

A

B

55

Shelves

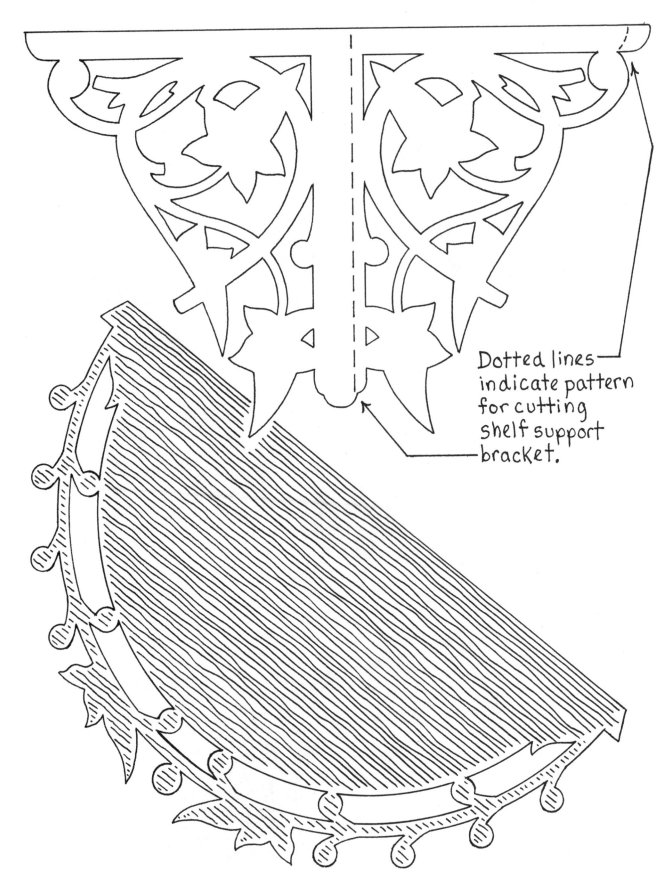

Dotted lines
indicate pattern
for cutting
shelf support
bracket.

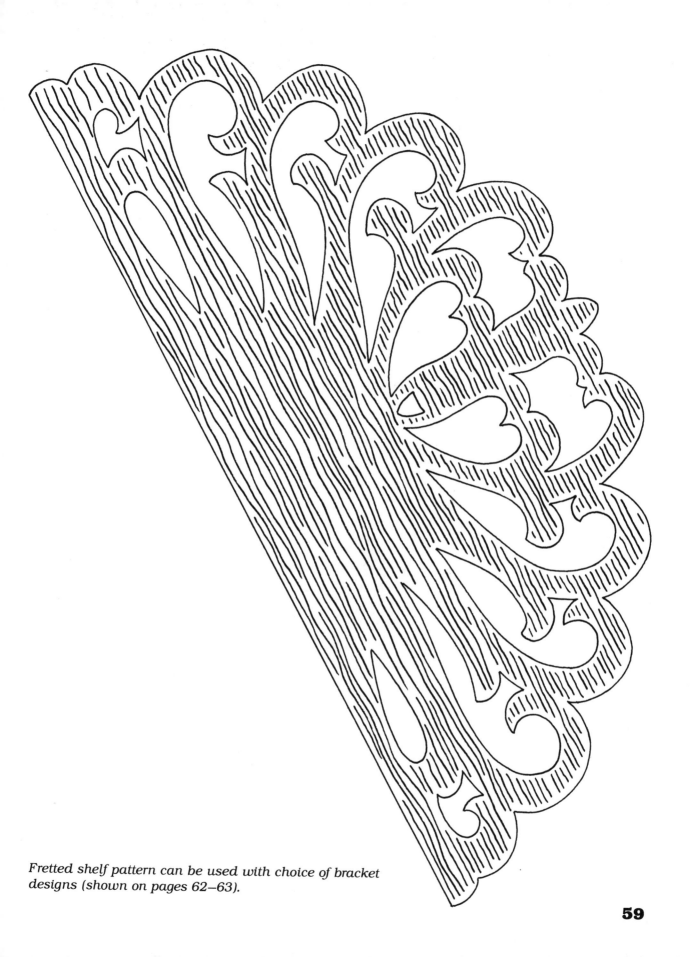

Fretted shelf pattern can be used with choice of bracket designs (shown on pages 62–63).

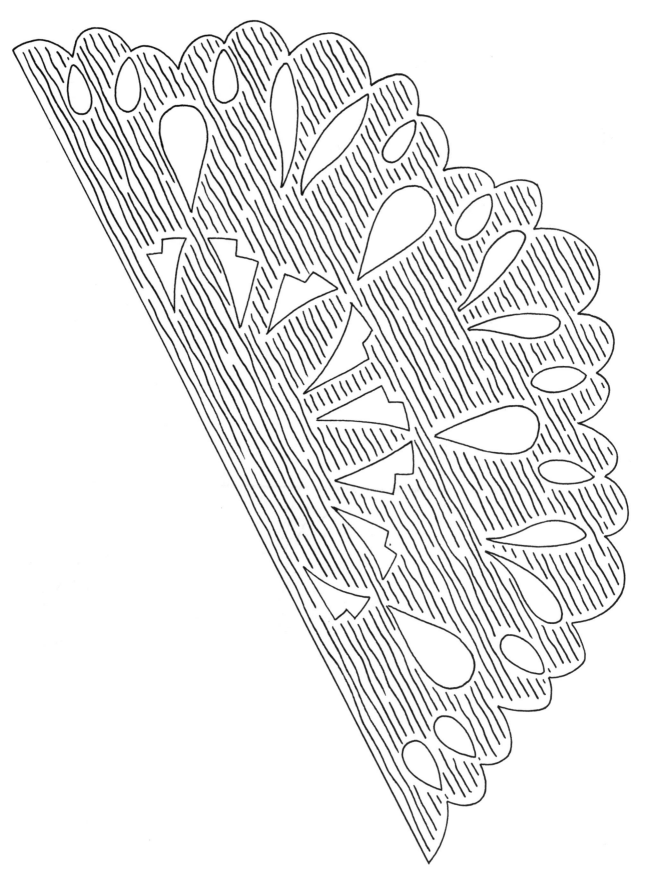

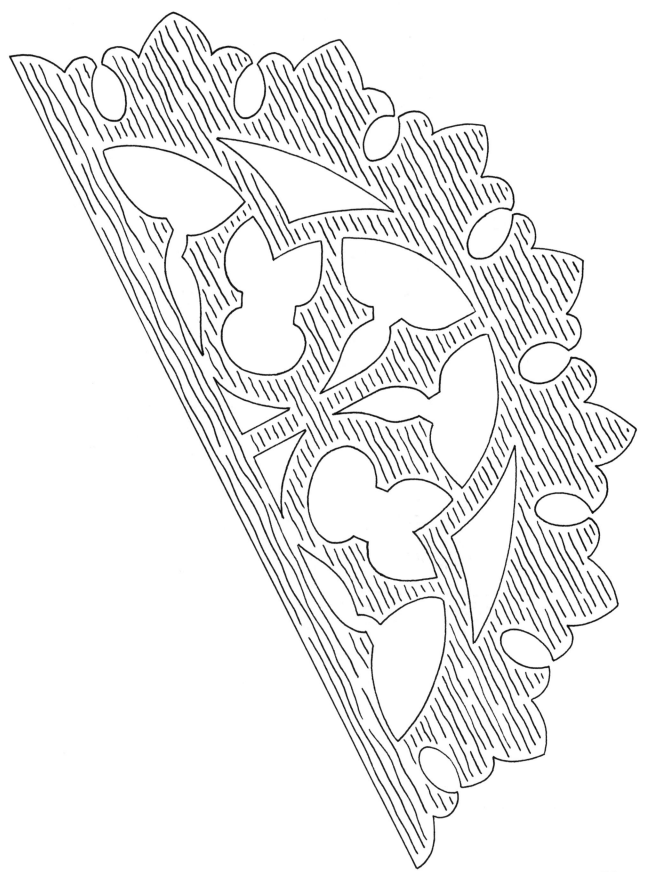

61

Bracket pattern can be used with choice of wall shelf patterns (shown on pages 59–61).

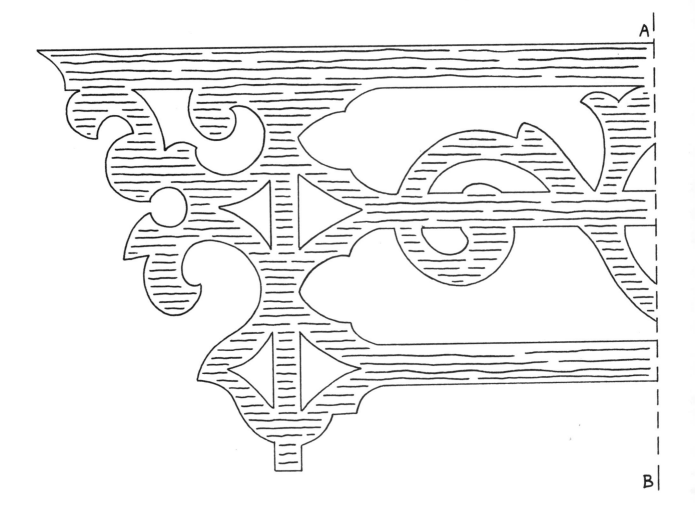

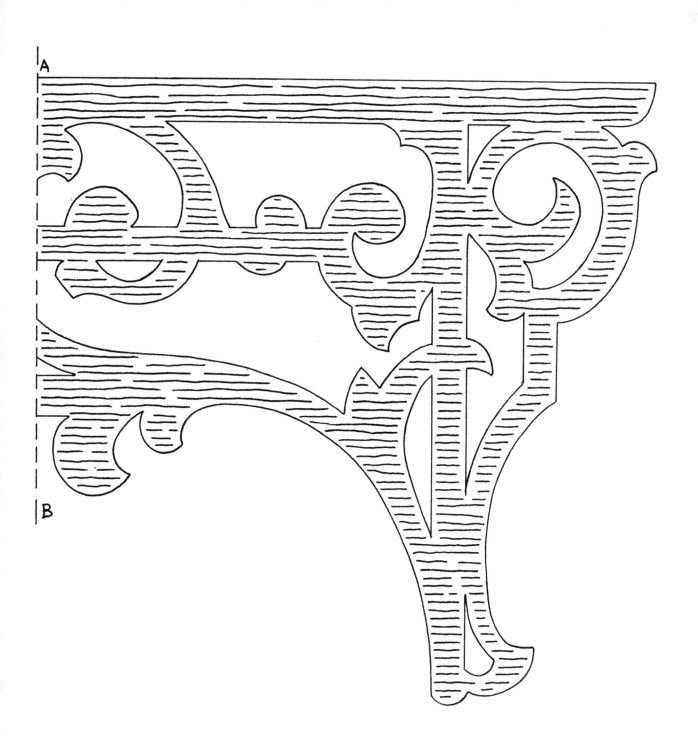

A

B

65

B A A B

68

A   B

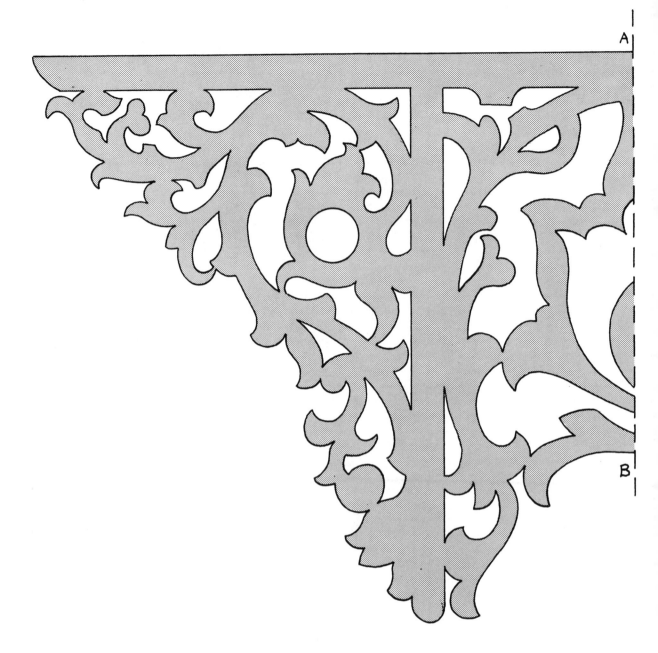

A

B

A

D

C

75

A

B

76

A

B

B

A

78

B

A

A

B

C_L

A

B

81

A

B

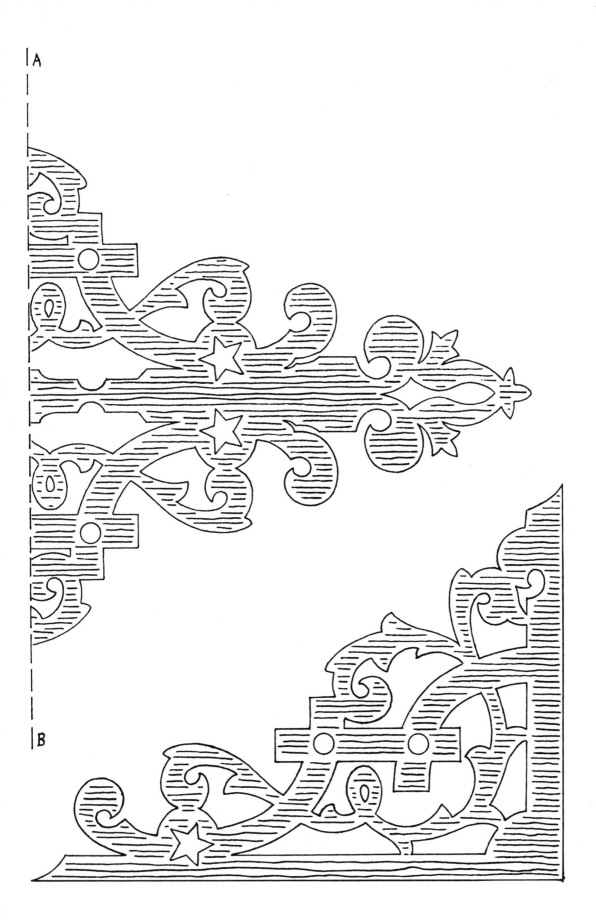

A

B

83

A

B

84

A

B

Picture/Mirror Frames

Quarter pattern for large frame.

C

Large frame with mirror sawn from ¾-inch solid oak.

B

A

Quarter pattern for large frame.

B A

C

Quarter pattern for large frame.

98

A

B

C

Quarter pattern for large frame.

A

B

A

B

A

B

A

B

103

A

B

A

REAR SUPPORT FOR
STANDING FRAME
Attach with metal hinge or small
piece of fabric or leather fastened
to top of support and back of frame

B

105

A

B

A

B

A

B

A

B

109

A

B

110

A

B

₵L

111

A

B

A

B

FANCY PHOTO FRAME

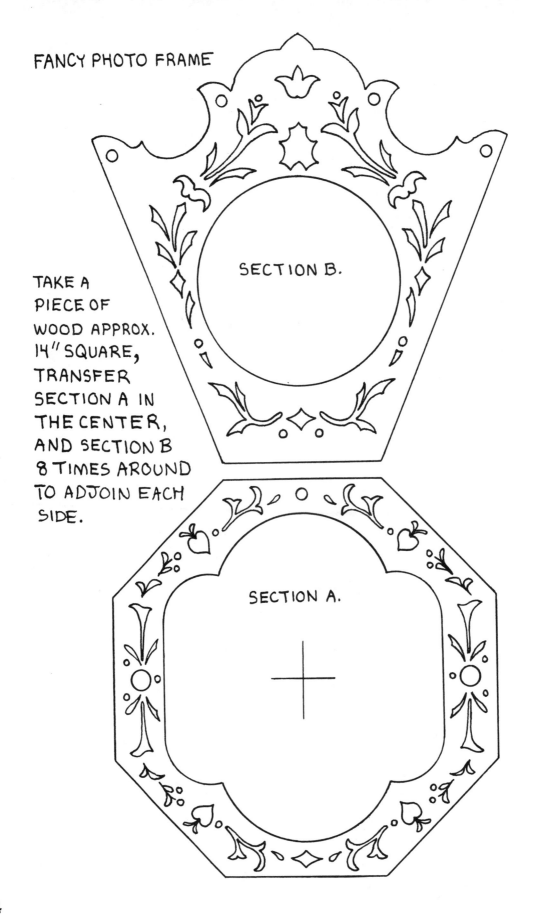

SECTION B.

TAKE A
PIECE OF
WOOD APPROX.
14" SQUARE,
TRANSFER
SECTION A IN
THE CENTER,
AND SECTION B
8 TIMES AROUND
TO ADJOIN EACH
SIDE.

SECTION A.

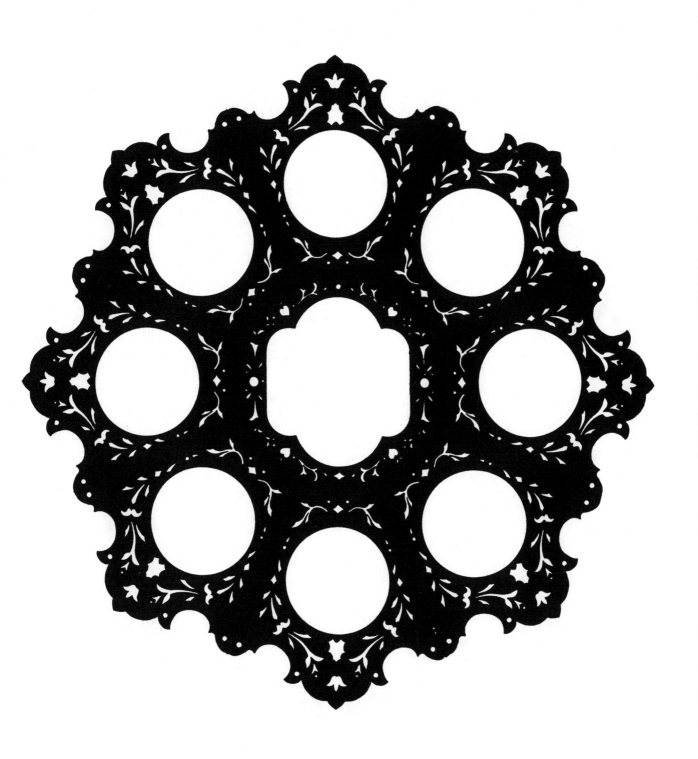

Snapshot frame. Here's what the parts as cut and assembled from the patterns on the previous page will look like.

Table Mat

END PANELS ~ Make 2

A

A   B

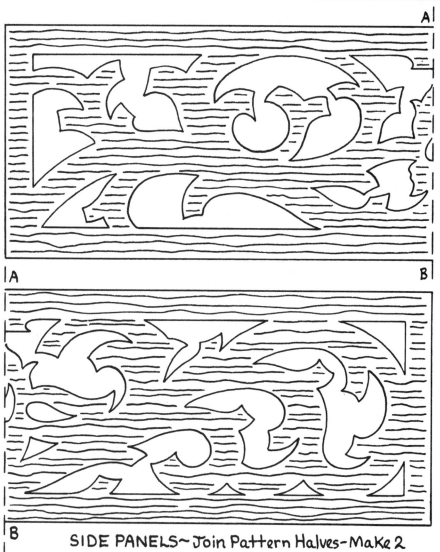

B

SIDE PANELS ~ Join Pattern Halves ~ Make 2

WORK BOX — Join Pattern Halves — Make 2 For
Top & Bottom Panels

A

B

118

A

B

119

TOP

END ~ Make 2

← SIDES FOR TOP
Make 2
Bevel/Mitre Edges
Of All Top Parts
For Optimum Results.

Interior Of Box May
Be Lined And Padded
With Fabric.

END FOR TOP ~ Make 2

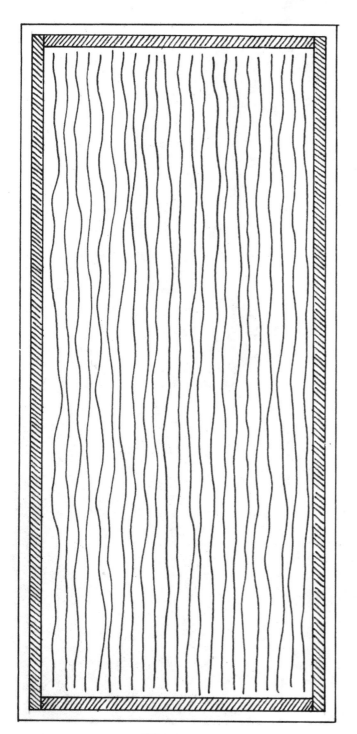

BASE

SIDE ~ Make 2

Hanging Match Box

Side

Bottom

Side

Roof Panels →
Cut 2

Thermometer Stand

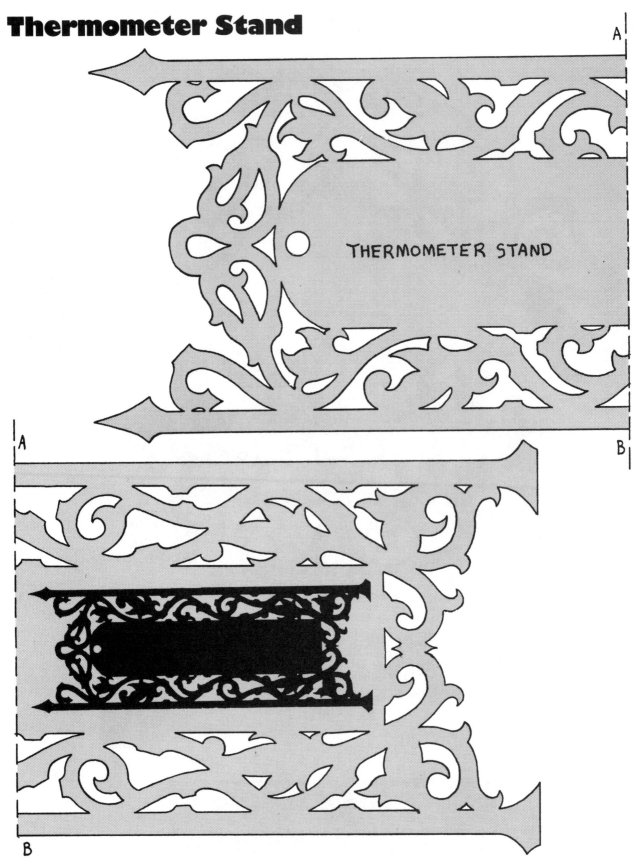

THERMOMETER STAND

Doll's Bedstead

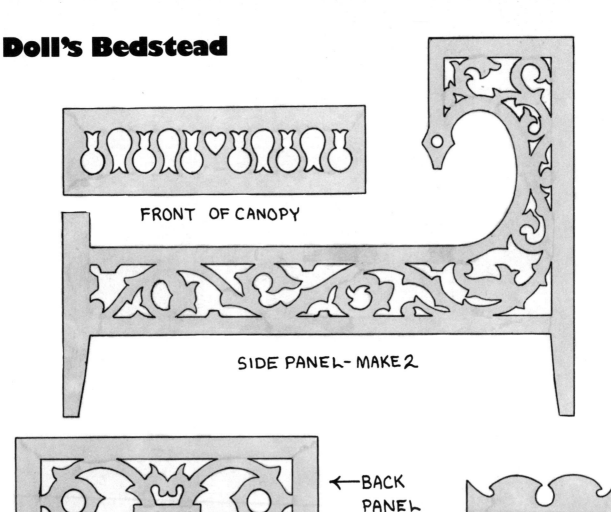

FRONT OF CANOPY

SIDE PANEL—MAKE 2

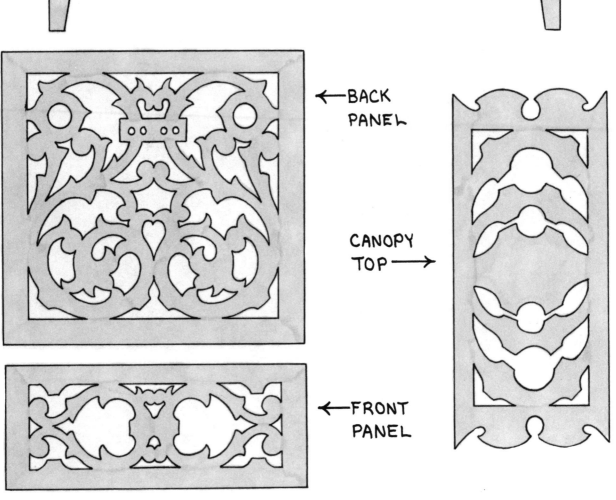

← BACK PANEL

CANOPY TOP →

← FRONT PANEL

MINIATURE
TABLE
Use $\frac{1}{8}$" thick
material.

LEGS ──→
Make 2 and
divide one
in the
middle, then
fit to each
side.

TOP ──→

Wall Pockets

Use cloth for sides.
Drape with tassels.
Hang against wall.

WALL POCKET
Use $\frac{1}{8}$" Thick Material

BACK PANEL

CUT A BOTTOM PANEL 4" x $\frac{7}{8}$"

← SIDES →

FRONT PANEL

129

Fancy work box, wall pocket.

FANCY WORK BOX

SIDES—
make 2

BOTTOM →

130

A

ENDS—Make 2

B

Baskets

WORK BASKET~ BOTTOM PANEL

SIDE VIEW

END VIEW

WORK BASKET
END PANEL (Make 2)

Work basket for holding photos, knives, spoons and utensils.

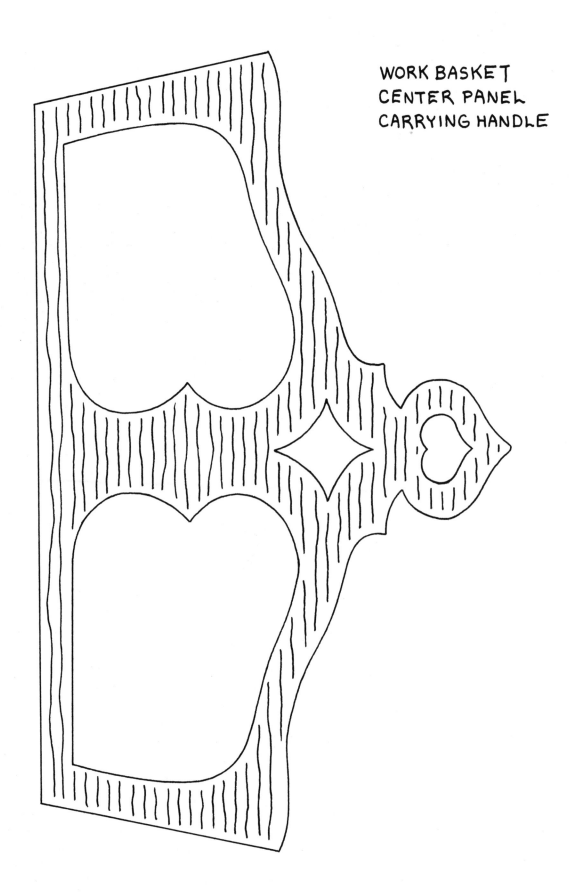

WORK BASKET
CENTER PANEL
CARRYING HANDLE

WORK BASKET
Make from $\frac{1}{4}''$
thick material

SIDE PANEL
(Make 2)

FRUIT BASKET
BASE

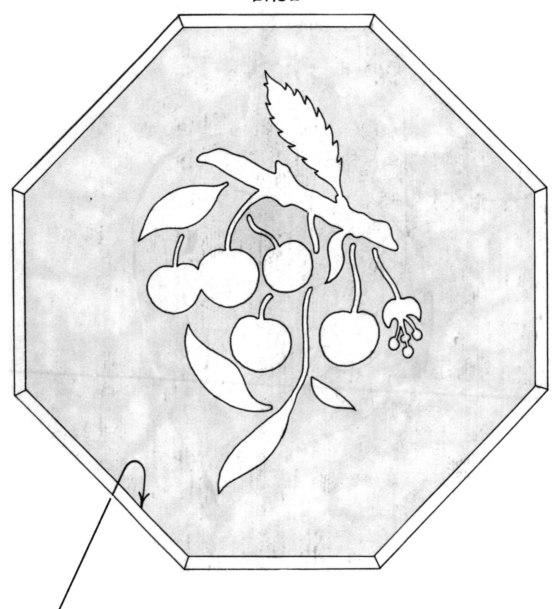

CUT ON INSIDE LINE TO PRODUCE BASE
For Perfect Fit, Bevel Edges Of Base To
Angle Of Side Pieces.
Side Pieces Attach To Outer Edge Of Base.

SIDE PANELS — Make 4 Of Each And Alternate Pieces

END VIEWS ~ Bevel Edges

FANCY BASKET ON STAND

BOTTOM PIECE

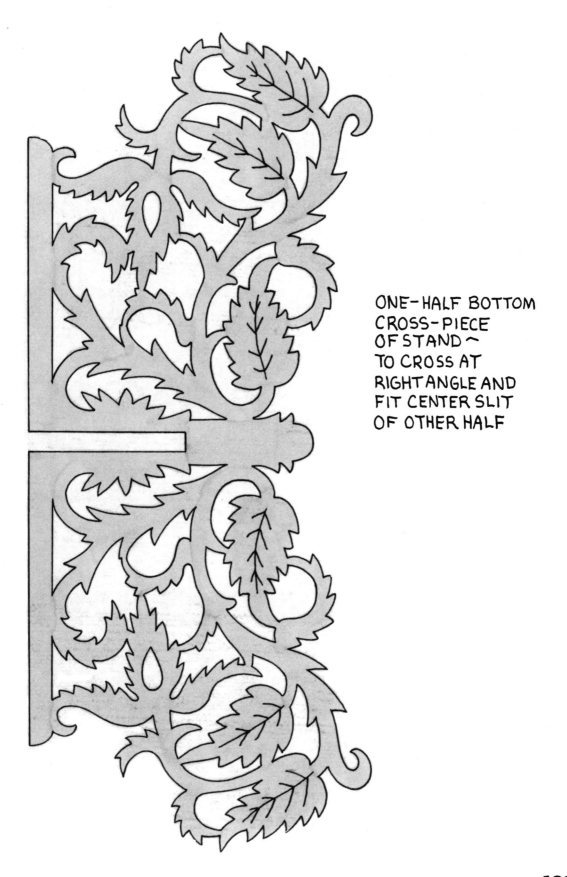

ONE-HALF BOTTOM
CROSS-PIECE
OF STAND ~
TO CROSS AT
RIGHT ANGLE AND
FIT CENTER SLIT
OF OTHER HALF

SIDE PIECES FOR TOP
CUT EIGHT TIMES

SIDE PIECES FOR EDGE
CUT EIGHT TIMES

A

B

A

B

143

WORK BASKET BOTTOM~ $\frac{1}{2}$ PATTERN

FANCY BASKET

End Pieces
(Cut 2)

Side Panel (Cut 2)

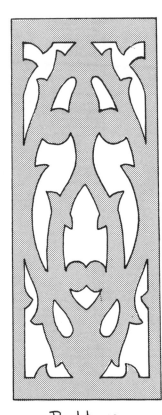

Bottom

Ink Stand and Pen Holder

Suggested Material ~ $\frac{1}{4}''$ Thickness

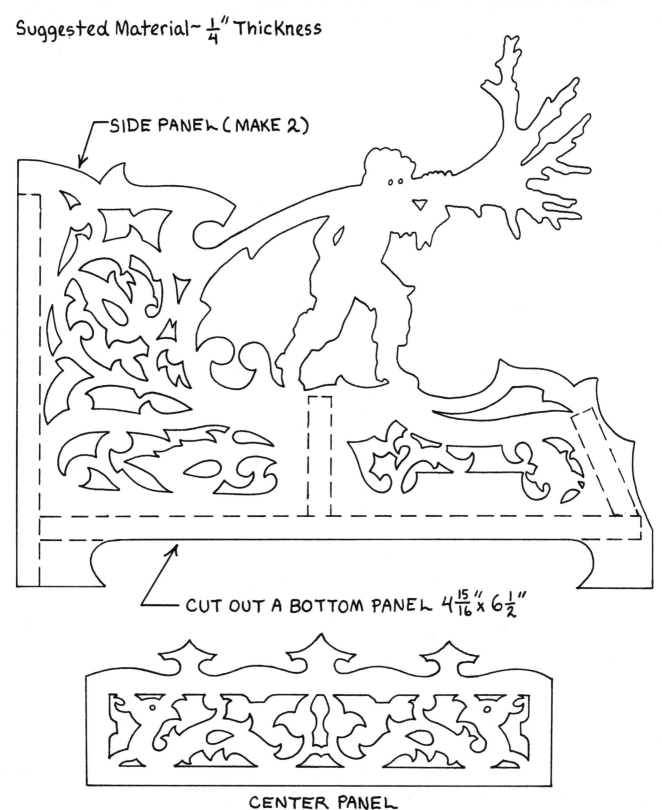

SIDE PANEL (MAKE 2)

CUT OUT A BOTTOM PANEL $4\frac{15}{16}'' \times 6\frac{1}{2}''$

CENTER PANEL

INKSTAND
BACK PANEL

FRONT PANEL

END VIEW

BEVEL BOTTOM

Plant Hanger

Plant hanger of solid walnut is a fun and interesting project. Six identical vertical pieces of ¼"-thick material are uniquely hinged together and surround two turnings. The notched round base or shelf holds the entire assembly together. It is easily disassembled for flat storage.

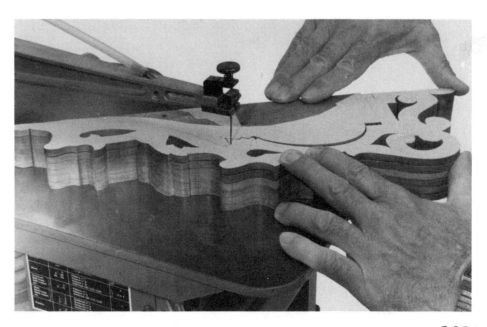

A good scroll saw will cut all six layers at once as shown here.

All the parts, sawn, turned, sanded, and finished. Note the screw eye in the turned member at the right. This is the only metal fastener used in this project.

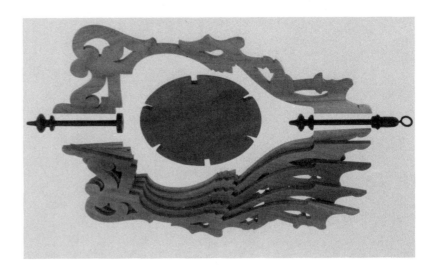

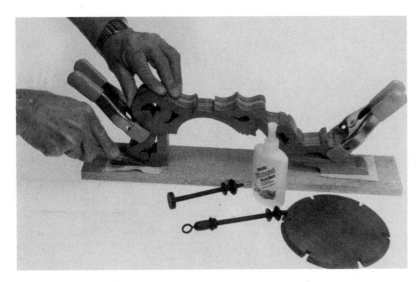

Two pieces of fabric, such as light canvas or denim, are used to hinge the six vertical pieces together. Clamp the wood parts and glue them to the fabric as shown. When the glue has set, trim the excess fabric away with a knife.

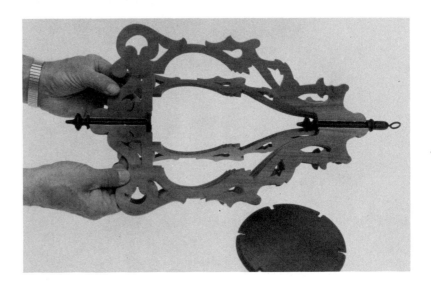

Assembly of the plant hanger project. The six vertical pieces wrap around the turnings on the fabric hinge. The notched base locks all the pieces together.

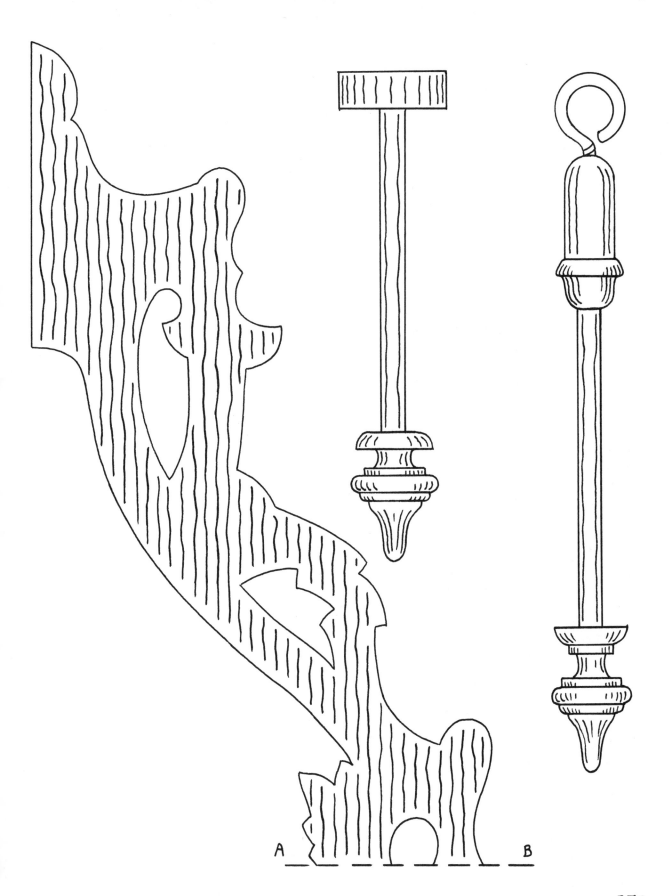

A

B

151

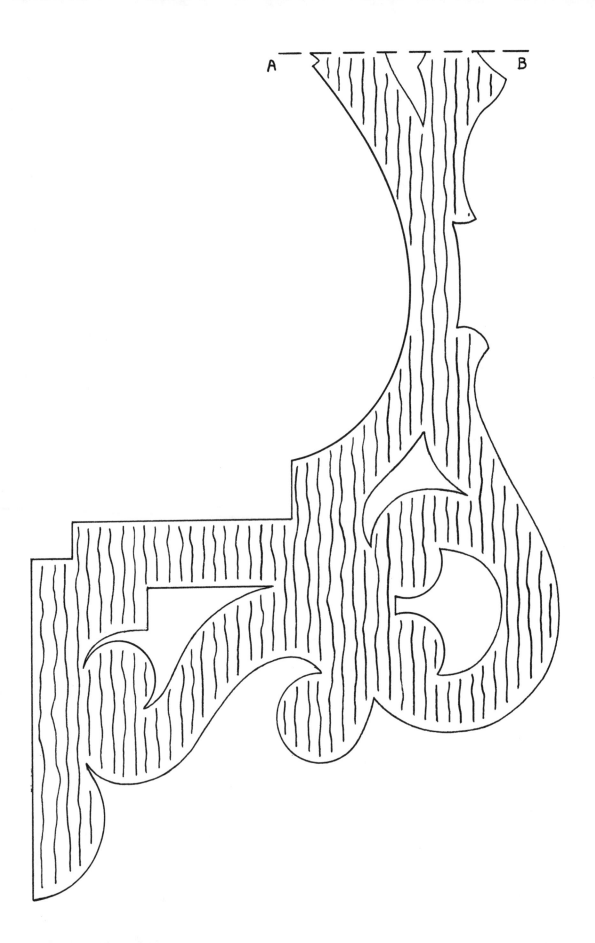

A   B

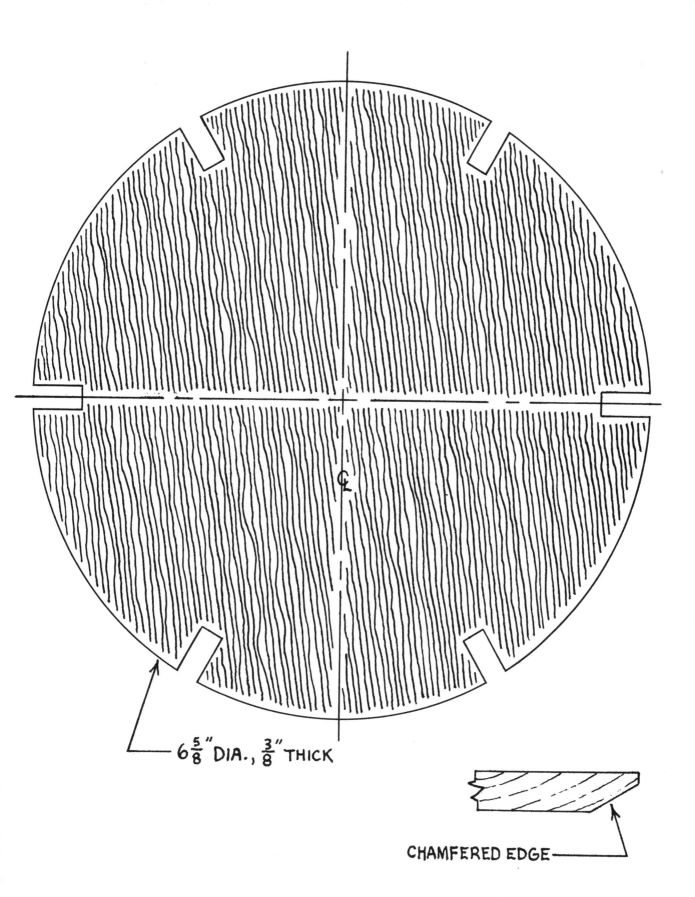

$6\frac{5}{8}''$ DIA., $\frac{3}{8}''$ THICK

CHAMFERED EDGE

Potpourri

156

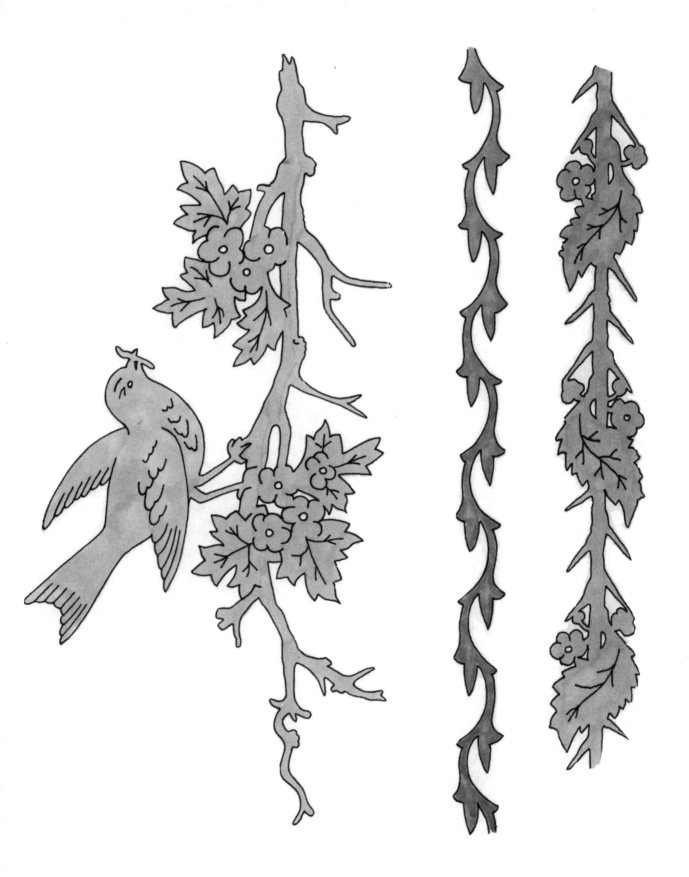

157

About the Author

Patrick Spielman's love of wood began when, as a child, he transformed fruit crates into toys. Now this prolific and innovative woodworker is respected worldwide as a teacher and author.

His most famous contribution to the woodworking field has been his perfection of a method to season green wood with polyethylene glycol 1000 (PEG). He went on to invent, manufacture, and distribute the PEG-Thermovat chemical seasoning system.

During his many years as a shop instructor in Wisconsin, Spielman published manuals, teaching guides, and more than 14 popular books, including *Modern Wood Technology*, a college text. He also wrote six educational series on wood technology, tool use, processing techniques, design, and wood-product planning.

Author of the best-selling *Router Handbook* (over three-quarters of a million copies sold), Spielman has served as editorial consultant to a professional magazine, and his products, techniques, and many books have been featured in numerous periodicals.

This pioneer of new ideas and inventor of countless jigs, fixtures, and designs used throughout the world is a unique combination of expert woodworker and brilliant teacher—all of which endear him to his many readers and to his publisher.

At Spielmans Wood Works in the woods of northern Door County, Wisconsin, he and his family create and sell some of the most durable and popular furniture products and designs available.

Should you wish to write, please forward your letters to Sterling Publishing Company, Inc.

CHARLES NURNBERG
STERLING PUBLISHING COMPANY, INC.

Current Books by Patrick Spielman

Alphabets and Designs for Wood Signs. 50 alphabet patterns, plans for many decorative designs, the latest on hand carving, routing, cutouts, and sandblasting. Pricing data. Photo gallery (4 pages in color) of wood signs by professionals from across the U.S. Over 200 illustrations. 128 pages.

Carving Large Birds. Spielman and renowned woodcarver Bill Dehos show how to carve a fascinating array of large birds. All of the tools and basic techniques that are used are discussed in depth, and hundreds of photos, illustrations, and patterns are provided for many graceful birds. Oversized. 16 pages in full color. 192 pages.

Carving Wild Animals: Life-Size Wood Figures. Spielman and renowned woodcarver Bill Dehos show how to carve more than 20 magnificent creatures of the North American wild. Step-by-step, photo-filled instructions and multiple-view patterns, plus tips on the use of tools, wood selection, finishing, and polishing help you bring each animal to life. Oversized. Over 300 photos; 16 pages in full color. 240 pages.

Gluing & Clamping. A thorough, up-to-date examination of one of the most critical steps in woodworking. Spielman explores the features of every type of glue—from traditional animal-hide glues to the newest epoxies—the clamps and tools needed, the bonding properties of different wood species, safety tips, and all techniques. Also included is a glossary of terms. Over 500 illustrations. 256 pages.

Making Country-Rustic Wood Projects. Hundreds of photos, patterns, and detailed scaled drawings reveal construction methods, woodworking techniques, and Spielman's professional secrets for making indoor and outdoor furniture in the distinctly attractive country-rustic style. Covered are all aspects of furniture making from choosing the best wood for the job to texturing smooth boards. Among the dozens of projects are mailboxes, cabinets, and many other durable and economical pieces. 400 illustrations. 4 pages in full color. 164 pages.

Making Wood Decoys. A clear step-by-step approach to the basics of decoy carving, abundantly illustrated with closeup photos. Six different professional decoy artists are featured. Photo gallery (4 pages in full color) along with numerous detailed plans for various popular decoys. 160 pages.

Making Wood Signs. Designing, selecting woods and tools, and every process through finishing are clearly covered. Hand-carved, power-carved, routed, and sandblasted processes in small to huge signs are presented. Foolproof guides for professional letters and ornaments. Hundreds of photos (4 pages in full color). Lists sources for supplies and special tooling. 144 pages.

Realistic Decoys. Spielman and master carver Keith Bridenhagen reveal their successful techniques for carving, feather-texturing, painting, and finishing wood decoys. Details that you can't find elsewhere make this book invaluable. Includes listings for contests, shows, and sources of tools and supplies. 274 closeup photos, 28 in color. 224 pages.

Router Handbook. With nearly 600 illustrations of every conceivable bit, attachment, jig, and fixture, plus every possible operation, this definitive guide has revolutionized router applications. It covers safety and maintenance tips, dovetailing, free-handing, advanced duplication, and more. Details for over 50 projects are included. 224 pages.

Router Jigs & Techniques. A practical encyclopedia of information, covering the latest equipment to use with your router, it describes jigs, bits, and other aids and devices. The book not only provides invaluable tips on how to determine the router and bits best suited to your needs, but tells you how to get the most out of your equipment once it is bought. Over 800 photos and illustrations. 384 pages.

Scroll Saw Country Patterns. The acknowledged master of the scroll saw presents a new selection of fresh, exciting patterns. The range of these projects is limitless, and Spielman gives you excellent instruction every step of the way. 400 patterns in 28 different categories.

Scroll Saw Handbook. This companion volume to *Scroll Saw Pattern Book* covers the essentials of this versatile tool, including the basics (how scroll saws work, blades to use, etc.) and the advantages and disadvantages of the general types and specific brand-name models available on the market. All cutting techniques are detailed, including compound and bevel sawing, making inlays, reliefs, and recesses. There's even a section on transferring patterns to wood! Over 500 illustrations. 256 pages.

Scroll Saw Fretwork Patterns. This companion book to *Scroll Saw Fretwork Techniques and Projects* features over 200 fabulous full-size fretwork patterns. These patterns include the most popular classic designs of the past, plus an array of imaginative contemporary ones. 256 pages.

Scroll Saw Fretwork Techniques and Projects. Spielman and master woodworker Reidle team up to make fretwork a quick and easy skill for anyone with access to a scroll saw, explaining every intricate detail in easy-to-follow instructions, photos, and drawings. Patterns for dozens of projects make it easy for any scroll saw user to master these designs. 232 pages (8 in color).

Scroll Saw Pattern Book. This companion book to *Scroll Saw Handbook* contains over 450 workable patterns for making wall plaques, refrigerator magnets, candle holders, and many more projects. Beginners and experienced scroll sawyers alike will be challenged. 256 pages.

Scroll Saw Puzzle Patterns. 80 full-size patterns for jigsaw puzzles, standup puzzles and inlay puzzles. With meticulous attention to detail, Patrick and Patricia Spielman provide instruction and step-by-step photos, along with tips on tools and wood selections, for making standup puzzles. Inlay puzzle patterns include basic shapes, numbers, an accurate piece-together map of the United States and a host of other colorful, educational and enjoyable games for children. 8 pages of color. 256 pages.

Spielman's Original Scroll Saw Patterns. Patrick Spielman has teamed up with his wife, Patricia, on this all-new book of scroll saw patterns, with projects covering over 30 different categories. Each step is clearly spelled out, with hundreds of photos and drawings that show you how to flop, repeat, and crop each design for thousands of variations. 224 pages.

Working Green Wood with PEG. Covers every process for making beautiful, inexpensive projects from green wood without cracking, splitting, or warping. Hundreds of clear photos and drawings show every step. 175 unusual project ideas. Lists supply stores. 160 pages.

Index